25. 5. 79.

Tie·dye, Batik and Candlemaking

In easy steps

Tie-dye, Batik

and Candlemaking
In easy steps

Norma Jameson and
Ann Hirst-Smith

Studio Vista
London

Written by Norma Jameson (pages 6-32)
and Ann Hirst-Smith (pages 33-63)

Photographs by Peter Hirst-Smith

A Studio Vista book published by
Cassell & Collier Macmillan Publishers Ltd.,
35 Red Lion Square, London WC1R 4SG
and at Sydney, Auckland, Toronto, Johannesburg,
an affiliate of
Macmillan Publishing Co. Inc.
New York.

Copyright © Studio Vista 1976
First published in 1976

ISBN 0 289 70723 4

Set in Times Roman by RSB Photosetting, Lightwater, Surrey, England.

Printed in The Netherlands by Smeets Offset, Weert.

Contents

1 Put the dye mixture into cold water with salt and then washing soda and stir well.

2 Tie an ordinary single knot fairly tightly in the centre of a piece of cloth.

Introduction to Tie-dye

All the equipment you will need to make the tie-dye projects in this book. *Hot or cold water powder dyes* – these are obtainable from department stores and the instructions included should be followed carefully, with the one exception that instead of rinsing fabric immediately after dyeing as most instructions recommend it is advisable to let the material dry for 24 hours beforehand. Rinse in cold water to remove surplus dye and remember that cloth can only take up a certain amount of dye at one time so don't be alarmed if the rinsing water becomes highly coloured. *Salt solution and washing soda solution* – these fix the dye. *A mixing bowl* for the dye solution. *Rubber gloves* for protection. *An iron* to remove the creases made in the material by tight bindings. *Scissors. Needles and thread* for the sewn hanging (15). *Raffia, string, elastic bands, cotton thread* – these are tied around the cloth to prevent the dye from entering the fibres. Make sure the tie of binding is tight and secure. Elastic bands are the quickest and easiest bindings to use. *Small objects* such as dried peas, cotton reels, buttons, shells, pebbles, marbles, corks, rice, pieces of dowel rod or blocks of wood – these are bound inside the cloth to make shapes of different sizes and add an element of surprise when undoing the ties after dyeing. *Small pieces of clear plastic bag* to protect selected areas of the cloth from the dye.

You don't have to be an expert to practise the art of tie-dye. It is a simple and easy method of decorating cloth with a variety of patterns made from spots, circles, spirals, stripes and patches in simple or complex arrangements. Anyone with strong and nimble fingers and an eye for colour can produce beautiful and original fabrics.

Tie-dye, as its name implies, is a method by which material is tied or bound before it is dyed so that the pressure of the tie or binding excludes the liquid dye when the cloth is immersed. Suitable materials to use are medium and fine cotton, silk and wool. Use old pieces of cotton cloth such as sheets and handkerchiefs for your experiments and remember that all material should be washed before dyeing. Materials with crease-resisting properties or synthetic mixtures are not suitable as dye will not penetrate the fibres of the cloth evenly.

In tie-dye in its simplest form the cloth itself can be tied in knots tight enough to prevent dye from penetrating them. This method forms exciting irregular patterns when the cloth is unknotted. Knot at random over an area of the cloth for a variety of circular splashes or along a length of material for a zigzag striped effect. With this 'direct knotting' method make the dye fairly concentrated and dip the cloth in and out very quickly so the dye does not have time to penetrate the cloth within the knots.

Having experimented with the simplest form of tie-dye you will be ready to try the exciting projects which follow using a variety of the ties and bindings illustrated on page 6. Every different binding produces its own slight variation on a theme and it is well worth analysing these patterns and noting them for future reference.

If you enjoy tie-dye you will certainly enjoy batik! Both methods have qualities in common. They are both resist techniques and, most importantly, they both provide a direct method of producing exclusive patterned fabrics.

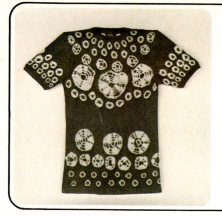

T-Shirt

1 Make a drawing of the T-shirt showing possible designs and relative sizes of the circles.

2 Draw the basic design roughly on the T-shirt with charcoal or pastel.

3 Place dried peas in the centre of all circles, and bind them securely with an elastic band.

4 When all the pattern is tied up securely, check that no part of the design has been missed.

You will need:
Plain cotton T-shirt
Charcoal, soft pencil or pastel
Dried peas
Elastic bands
Olive green dye

It is a good idea to have some basic design in mind when tie-dyeing clothes. Make quick drawings of ideas to give some indication of the finished result. These drawings need not be accurate but if you feel able to jot down a series of possibilities it might help you to choose the design.

White cotton T-shirts can be decorated easily. By using the simplest form of tying and only one dye the pattern appears in white against one colour. In this case it is better to use a dark, contrasting colour to show the pattern clearly. For first experiments and designs single dyeings against white show the effect quickly.

Dyeing
This T-shirt was dyed olive green in Procion M dye. These dyes are in powder form and are strong. They are easy to mix and to use and are colour and light fast. Mix five tablespoons of salt in cold water in one container and in

another, mix two tablespoons of washing soda with hot water to dissolve it quickly. To obtain a dark green mix two heaped teaspoons of dye to a paste with a little cold water in a small glass jar. Then fill the jar with hot water. Put enough cold water in a plastic bowl to cover the T-shirt easily. Next, put the mixed liquid dye into the water, followed by the salt mixture and then the soda. Chemical reactions are set up by the addition of salt and soda which render the dye inactive after two hours.

If you have more than one piece of material to dye it is a good idea to wait until all the designs are completed before mixing the dye. If you want them all the same depth of colour they must all be plunged in the dye together and turned frequently to make sure the material is dyed evenly all over. If this is not required, the articles can be put in one after the other, in which case the first article will usually dye a deeper tone than the successive articles.

These Procion M dyes have a great advantage over most other dyes in that they are fixed, or made permanent, just by being hung up or left on newspaper in a warm room for 24 hours. Rinse them in cold water to remove loose particles of dye, wash in hot soapy water, and rinse again; then iron in the usual way.

Creases caused by tight tying can be ironed out while the article is still damp.

Patterns like this are reminiscent of markings on animal skins. The circles and diamond shapes could be used as ideas for making patterned material to be made into soft toys; for example snakes would look very realistic with coloured diamond shapes along the back.

5 Immerse the article quickly in the bowl of dye; turn it repeatedly to ensure even dyeing.

6 Remove bands from the dry T-shirt revealing the white circles against the green background.

Cushion Covers

1 To begin a series of concentric circles, pick up the centre of the cloth and bind securely.

2 To make several circles, add more bindings leaving suitable spaces between each tie.

3 If you want pieces of material to match in colour, bind and dye them at the same time.

You will need:
Sufficient cotton to cover your
  cushion, cut to size
Elastic bands
Raffia
Orange, red, blue and green dyes

There are many ways of using tie-dyed material. One of the easiest is to make colourful covers for cushions. A circular form within a square is a good structure on which to base ideas. It can be varied in width of circle and width of space between the circles and can be one circle or many circles. It can eventually grow into a spiral form from the centre of the cushion. The circles themselves can be concentric or separate, floating about in space and not connected. They can be all the same size or irregular in size. The cushion itself can be circular, in which case the circle patterns could echo the edge of the cushion, overlap, or interlock. The number of designs based on the circle is limitless. Experiment and try out a series of variations based on the placing of circles.

Today there seems to be a return to pattern. Colourful sheets have taken the place of the old pure white. Pillowcases are patterned to match sheets, covers and curtains. All these can be decorated by the tie-dye method, as long as they are not made of synthetic materials.

It should be remembered when tying up the cloth that dye penetrates the fibres of fine material more quickly than those of heavier material. Sheets and curtains may need longer immersion in the dye for it to go through to the innermost folds of the cloth.

Do not be disappointed if, when you undo the circle ties, only sections of the circles have dyed. All

4 When the first dye is dry, you may add more bindings between the others to resist the next dye.

5 Remove the bindings and rinse, wash and iron the cloth. White and orange circles appear on red.

6 More bindings have been added and the cloth dyed olive green. This changes red into brown.

7 Remove all the bindings, wash the cloth, iron it, re-bind it spirally and dye it green.

you need to do is to re-tie them making sure that the cloth which did not dye the first time is on the outside of the tie to take the second dye. This happened on the cushion design using the four separate pieces. After dyeing in orange and red too much white was left so all four pieces of cloth were re-tied and dyed in blue. Some overlapping of colours took place, turning some of the red into purple and some orange to brown. Accidents can very often be turned to good effect as long as you re-dye your material in a complementary colour.

11

Scarves

1 Dye the material blue and dry it. Fold it into accordion pleats and iron to make the folds crisp.

2 Untie the cloth after the first binding to check the quality of the second, darker blue.

You will need:
Old scarves, cotton squares or a
    long length of cotton lawn
Iron
Raffia
Blue, orange, green and pink dyes

Experiments on odd or old bits of plain material often produce positive and exciting results which can be made up into something useful. Old silk squares or long scarves which need a face lift often provide opportunities for taking risks with new or expensive materials. If you use an old piece of material you take a slight risk if

3 Add more bindings and dye the cloth orange, which will change the blue to brown.

4 New bindings have been added to make more stripes. Dye the cloth green to darken the brown.

5 The cloth is untied, washed and ironed, to show the complete range of colours and stripes.

6 You can also decorate a long cloth with a ropemaker's twist. Hold one end and twist tightly.

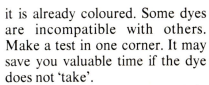

7 Fold the twist in half and the doubled strand will coil itself. Bind the two ends.

8 To make a more complicated pattern repeat the twisting and re-twisting and bind again.

it is already coloured. Some dyes are incompatible with others. Make a test in one corner. It may save you valuable time if the dye does not 'take'.

If the finished article is simple in shape complete any necessary sewing beforehand, then the stitching will take the dye at every stage.

Stripes and checks

The method of making regular stripes can be used in a straightforward way or modifications of the idea can be used to make repeated stripes or checks. If the material is turned round and folded at right angles to the previous stripes then re-dyed, squares will be formed. The material can be folded from corner to corner to form diagonal stripes.

Twisting

The twisting method illustrated is a way of producing subtle, textured bands across the material. Materials treated in this way provide good complementary backgrounds for overworking in other fabric techniques such as embroidery or batik.

9 Bind the resulting twists spirally. This creates pressure points which exclude the dye.

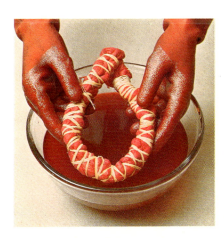

10 You can dye the twisted and bound scarf in a fairly small container (for about ten minutes).

Hangings

1 Drawing a basic idea for the final design helps to clarify the placing of the bindings

2 Draw the design onto the cloth, bind in the dried peas and dye the cloth pink.

3 When some bindings are completed, the cloth becomes distorted into fantastic shapes.

4 The same piece of material seen from below. Each binding diminishes the area of cloth.

5 The cloth is dyed blue to change pink to lilac. Check the tones frequently.

6 Use plastic bag pieces to protect areas from the dye, and make sure that they are firmly tied.

FIREWORKS
You will need:
Cotton fabric
Paper
Felt-tip pens
Dried peas
Elastic bands
Clear plastic bags
Raffia
Pink, pale blue and dark blue dyes

In addition to providing unusual materials for clothes and furnishings, the process of tie-dye can be used to make unique and colourful wall-hangings.

The characteristic of circular

7 The finished cloth is dyed in navy blue. Place it on a thick pad of newspaper to dry.

8 An exciting moment. Take out all the peas and bindings to reveal the final pattern.

ties is that they resemble suns, stars, explosions, fireworks and so it seems logical to exploit this when designing. It is often possible to begin an idea this way and let the design grow from colour to colour without a preconceived idea of the end product.

In this wall-hanging the method of tying spots and circles clustered together was employed to indicate the explosions of colourful fireworks against a dark sky.

When choosing a series of colours for a wall-hanging of this kind the nature of the subject should be taken into account. Fireworks often make pink, white and silver lights against the sky so a colour progression was chosen to suit the subject based on pink through to lilac and then to deep midnight blue.

Experiment with colours to see what happens when one is dyed over another.

SEWN HANGING
You will need:
Cotton fabric
Soft pencil
Ruler
Needle and strong thread
Pins
Orange, blue and green dyes

African women use this sewing technique to decorate large cloths in indigo dye. Their patterns are strong and simple in design. Cotton thread and raffia can be used for the stitching. The cloth can be folded and over-stitched to exclude the dye. It can be basted and the basting stitches can be pulled up very tightly to gather the cloth together so that the dye partially penetrates the gathers. Many complicated designs can be made in this way from abstract stripes and circles to involved flower forms and animal patterns. The more elaborate patterns should

9 Draw lines on the cloth with a pencil and a ruler to mark where the sewn lines should go.

10 Tie a knot at the end of a length of strong thread before you begin to sew.

11 Pull up the thread when the sewing is completed and gather the cloth into uneven folds.

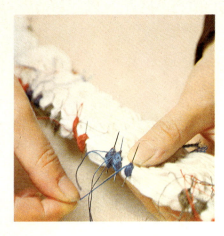

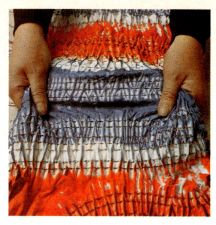

12 Pull the thread very tight and wind it in a figure 8 around a pin to stop it coming undone.

13 The cloth need not be totally submerged; it can be dip-dyed, dried, and dip-dyed again.

14 The threads are slackened to show the effect of dip-dyeing first in orange then in blue.

first be drawn onto the material so that the design can be kept under control. They can be drawn on the cloth faintly in pencil, charcoal or pastel which can be washed out at the end of the dyeing process.

This method of producing patterns is useful not only for making decorative wall-hangings but also lengths of material for articles of clothing. Although a more laborious method than the simple winding and binding technique it can produce more complex and controlled designs. A leaf shape, for example, will appear clearer if the outline of the leaf is basted onto the fabric before the cloth is dyed.

It is best to start with a fairly straightforward linear design (as in the sewn hanging) but once you have mastered this method there is no end to the exciting and original fabrics you can create.

Tablecloth

1 Experiment with tying different objects into the cloth: pebbles, blocks of wood, marbles.

2 The cloth has been dyed orange, red and brown. From below only one colour is seen.

3 Use sharp scissors to cut away the raffia. Remove all the objects and bindings.

You will need:
Square of cotton fabric, cut to size and hemmed
Small pebbles, dried peas, marbles, blocks of wood, buttons etc.
Elastic bands
Raffia
Orange, red and brown dyes

On special occasions the base or place-matted table gives way to a festival of colourful patterns. If all your table-cloths are white, try tying and dyeing one of them.

A large area of cloth like this is an ideal way to experiment with a lot of different objects and bind- ings – everything from dried peas and marbles to shells and small blocks of wood. Remember, also, that you can produce different effects by binding small pieces of clear plastic over areas of fabric to protect them from the dye.

Making a tie-dye tablecloth is also an ideal opportunity for a group project or a good party game. Persuade all your friends and the children to help and give everyone a section of cloth to tie up as they like. The process of un- tying provides fun and surprise. Each person who has taken part will want to identify his own per- sonal piece of 'cloth territory' and endeavour to remember which tie produced which effect. And com- parison of area with area will pro- vide much visual excitement.

When all the ties are undone and the cloth has been washed and ironed it is interesting to analyse the result. You will prob- ably find that no two shapes are the same.

Looking and analysing is a most important part of designing. Look at the natural colours, shapes and patterns in the world around you and you are sure to find many ideas.

Unusual Materials

1 Tie-dye supple suede like any other material, but use special dyes.

2 Removing the plastic bags from the dyed velvet. This shows the protected white areas.

For the bag, you will need:
Suitable piece of soft suede
Dried peas
Elastic bands
Brown suede dye
For the curtains:
Cotton velvet, cut to size and
 seamed where necessary
Raffia
Elastic bands
Clear plastic bags
Yellow and green dyes

Do not be afraid to try other more exotic materials such as wool, velvet, suede or nylon. Wool and velvet can be dyed with the usual cold and hot water dye, but suede must be dyed with special dye made for the purpose as also must nylon. Suitable dyes for these latter materials can now be bought in many department stores.

Suede
Of these four materials perhaps the most unusual to attempt to tie-dye is suede. Any suede can be printed and painted with special dyes but for tie-dyeing, it must be very soft and supple. If suede is hard it is impossible to control and dye seeps under the bindings. However, accidental seepage sometimes gives an unexpectedly

interesting quality. Here tie-dyed suede has been made up into an elegant evening bag.

Velvet
Velvet, too, is an exciting fabric to work with. It is almost impossible to imagine it tie-dyed but once you have tried it the richness and depth of colour will easily persuade you to explore its possibilities.

Sometimes when the ties are very tight the pile is flattened. Hanging in a hot steamy atmosphere for a few hours will usually remedy this.

Cotton velvet curtains
tie-dyed into sunbursts

Introduction to Batik

The basic principle of batik is that wax and liquid do not mix. This can be tried out with the simplest of equipment: a candle, a piece of cotton cloth, a bowl of dye and a pair of rubber gloves. Light the candle and allow it to drip onto the cloth. The wax dries almost instantly. Immerse the cloth in the bowl of dye and you will see that the patches where the candle has dripped will be white. The rest of the cloth will be dyed. This is the principle of all batik. Areas of cloth are protected by wax, and the material can be dyed, dried, waxed and dyed again repeatedly.

Other equipment will be necessary if you wish to experiment further. Blocks of paraffin wax are cheaper than candles. Some method of melting the wax is essential. Use either a double boiler or a saucepan part filled with water with a tin can inside it for the wax. Never let the saucepan boil dry because of fire risk. Perhaps the best solution is to invest in a thermostatically controlled heater. A deep-fat-fryer is ideal.

Various implements can be used to transfer the hot wax from the can to the cloth. A brush is the simplest. The traditional tools used by the Javanese, the tjanting and tjap, are more difficult to control but with practice the technique can be mastered. Other homemade mechanical aids are advantageous: template patterns, stencils and printing blocks.

Suitable materials for batik are pure cottons of all weights, linens and silks. Use old pieces of material to experiment. All materials, new or old, should be washed before they are dyed.

Dyeing
Unlike tie-dye cold water dyes must be used. Hot water would melt the wax off the material. Measuring spoons are essential, as is also a plastic bowl in which to mix the dye. When mixing dyes, follow the manufacturer's printed instructions.

Batik is an absorbing craft with many practical fashion and domestic applications. Its major attraction is that it is well within the capabilities of any reader with ideas and enthusiasm.

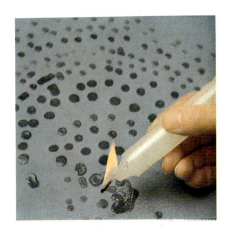

1 Allow a candle to drip onto the material in a spot or patch formation.

2 Dye in a dark blue; where the wax dripped remains pale blue and the background becomes darker.

Shirt

1 The tjanting is best used to make fine lines or spots and rhythmic, linear patterns.

2 Use a brush to paint larger areas of hot wax and to outline bold shapes.

You will need:
Pure cotton shirt
Cardboard
Tjanting
Brush
Melted wax
Yellow and purple dyes

Having learned the basic principles of batik you are now ready to embark on your first project. But first, a few words on how and when to remove the wax from your fabric.

When the dyeing processes are finished and the design is completed remove the wax by boiling the cloth for two, three or four minutes in a large saucepan or electric washing boiler, or by ironing out the wax between layers of absorbent paper. Then wash and rinse the material in the normal manner. It is then ready for use either as a decoration or to be made up into an article of clothing.

Once the wax has been removed by boiling, the fibres of the cloth will be back to normal and, if required, the process of waxing certain areas to retain parts of the pattern can be started again and the dyeing, drying and waxing can be repeated. These

'over dyeings' produce numerous permutations and changes in colour. It is fascinating to see the colourful images being formed by the addition of just one more dye. But be warned, learn when to stop.

The boiling off process does not have to be carried out after each dyeing. As many as three or four dyes can be put on before it is necessary to boil off. The wax cracks and deteriorates after this and begins to allow too much dye to seep under it. Watch it carefully – an otherwise good design can be spoiled if this happens.

When considering batik in relation to specific items of dress one must decide which is the most appropriate type of pattern. The choice lies between all-over texture, all-over pattern or single designs. For the shirt described in this section an homogeneous all-over texture was selected.

The traditional implements for batik are the brush (**1**), tjanting (**2**) or tjap (page 22), as already mentioned. But another interesting way of working, especially for a textured, all-over pattern on material is to cover the cloth completely with melted wax. Allow this to go cold and really hard;

3 Drip wax freely over the shirt. Place cardboard between back and front to stop sticking.

4 Dye the shirt yellow to add colour to the final pattern. Re-wax it all over.

5 Use firm pressure to crack the hardened wax sufficiently for the dye to seep into the cloth.

then by squeezing the cloth firmly, crack the wax all over. When it is plunged into the dye, turned and turned around and cracked yet again while submerged, the dye will seep into the hair-line cracks, and the result will be a covering of the cloth with a network of lines.

This technique can be combined with others to make textured backgrounds and is often used to link and unify patterns which may otherwise be too diverse. Cracking almost always occurs when a lot of wax has covered the material. This is characteristic of batik.

The cracking technique can be used with a single dye or numerous dyes. If the second method is required, after each successive dye the cracked wax must be re-waxed and then cracked again in different places. This means that the next dye will creep into these new cracks.

If the process is repeated several times, patterns or textures consisting of different coloured line networks will appear on the cloth. Once the material has been thickly waxed it may be difficult to remove the wax coating completely by only one boiling off, so do a further boiling.

Ties

1 Stamping blocks can be made from blocks of wood cut into a shape or nailed together.

2 Printing blocks can be made by knocking nails of various kinds into a block of wood.

3 A Javanese tjap made from copper strips is used for printing hot wax impressions onto cloth.

You will need:
Sufficient material to make a tie
Small blocks of wood
Nails
Sharp knife for carving wood
Tjanting
Melted wax
A selection of dyes

Stamping blocks, or 'tjaps' as they are called in Indonesia, are traditional implements used for stamping or printing melted wax on to cloth. These wax stampings form a resist to the cold dye and when the wax is removed, the pattern made by the block is left white and the rest of the cloth is coloured by the dye. Traditionally, tjaps are made of fine copper strips soldered together to form intricate patterns. Copper is used because it retains heat and keeps the wax liquid enough to enable the craftsman to print the design onto the cloth before the wax cools. Tjaps, which are quite heavy to use, are traditionally handled by the men of Java, while the women elaborate the formal and decorative patterns using tjantings.

Homemade stamping blocks can be made from odds and ends found in the garage and else-where: nuts, bolts, nails, copper pipe or carved wooden blocks. This brings us to the tricky matter of printing with tjap or block. Whatever type of block is used its printing surface must be held long enough in the hot wax to become hot itself otherwise the wax cools and becomes solid as soon as it is taken from the pot and before it can be printed on the cloth. Only one imprint should be made each time; one dip in the wax, and one print on the cloth. This keeps the print clear and the wax goes right through the fibres of the material.

4 A nail block, used to supplement the design made by the tjap, can make a subtle background.

5 Blocks can be used to make a free-flowing pattern or more formal, regular repeating patterns.

6 Four pieces of material made by using the traditional tjap and several homemade blocks.

This is essential for a clear print.

A shadow effect is obtained if the wax only goes partly through the cloth because the fibres at the back of the cloth are left unwaxed and will accept dye. The dye will penetrate only half the depth of the fibres and the resulting colour will be lighter than the rest of the dyed cloth. You can make use of this shadow technique.

Once a block is made it can be used in conjunction with other implements in the same way as the Javanese use the tjap blocks with a linking pattern made with a free-flowing tjanting on the same design. Combinations of these will produce endless variations.

Some blocks may come in useful for other designs at a later date. Do not discard them. Remember that it is the way in which you combine one block with another, or others, which produces widely differing effects.

Cotton was used for making the ties illustrated here but as you become more confident using the tjap and printing blocks you can try working with a fine fabric like silk. Silk must be treated with care, never boiled but heated gently to remove the wax.

23

Lampshade

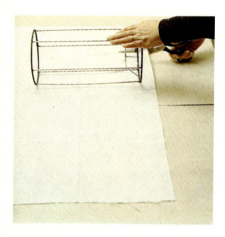

1 Roll the lamp base over the cloth to measure the amount of cloth needed.

2 Leave white spots to allow light to sparkle through. Some pink has been waxed.

3 The cloth is dyed blue to change the pink to lilac. There are now three colours.

You will need:
Lampshade frame (commercial, or an old frame you wish to re-cover)
Sufficient cloth to cover frame
Pins
Tjanting
Pink and blue dyes

Intricate details and colours in batiked material show to advantage with light shining through. This makes batiked material particularly suitable for making lampshades.

The lampshade is important in contemporary homes and for it to take its rightful place it should be planned to fit with its surroundings. Such planning involves careful consideration of the design of the lamp. It is necessary to take account of the shape, colour, and texture of the shade. The colour quality of light is perhaps the most important as it is this that creates atmosphere in a room. A warm glow is often considered to be the most successful quality to aim for. This is gained by using yellows, pinks or orange as foundation colours rather than cool colours, such as green and blue. Families of colours such as pinks, reds and purples or yellows, oranges and browns give ample scope for variety of design.

In a large lampshade bold designs are possible; the area of material is extensive enough to carry powerful designs. In a smaller shade, such as the one illustrated, a neater pattern is required as there is not much space for a free-flowing design. A spot pattern was decided upon, running vertically in irregular columns. Some emphasize white spots and other columns show pink spots as the most important element. They were joined by a

4 Wrap the finished cloth around the lamp base and pin it along the two edges.

5 Remove the cloth from its base and machine along the line of pins.

6 Cut the lower edge of the shade to echo the shape of the design, turn in and glue it down.

dark linking pattern which became pointed at the ends of each column forming a darker scalloped border at the top and bottom of the shade. When the material was put onto the frame the join proved satisfactory as it had been arranged so that the columns met easily and flowed into one another. This is usually a difficult problem to solve as the shrinkage of material cannot be calculated with absolute accuracy. It is therefore a good solution to plan a random design which is not difficult to join or to link across reasonably easily.

The shape of the base is equally important. A large base will look ridiculous with a small shade and a small base will look equally uncomfortable with a shade too large for it to balance. The colour of the base should also fit with the colour of the shade.

If you enjoy the effect of light through batiked fabric why not make your own blinds or shades out of heavy cotton or linen for your kitchen or bathroom. Combine the tjanting with a brush and printing blocks to create bold free-hand designs and remember to allow for shrinkage in your material when the fabric is boiled.

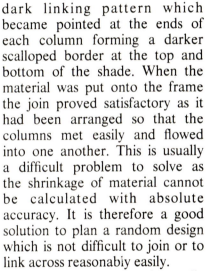

Wall Hangings

1 Draw stencil shapes and cut out strong cardboard. You can use them time and time again.

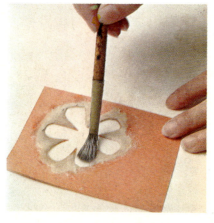

2 Place the stencil flat on the cloth, hold down firmly and brush wax from outside to centre.

3 The stencil is placed over the top of one of the pink flowers to enlarge it.

4 The stencil panel has been boiled off. The quality of colour is now more obvious.

GARDEN
You will need:
Cotton fabric
Strong cardboard
Soft pencil
Scissors or sharp cutting knife
Old newspaper
Brush
Melted wax
Pink, blue, green, purple and
    orange dyes

As well as being used for functional objects batik is an excellent medium for wall-hangings or pictures.

Stencils
A cut-out stencil is a useful device for producing either regular repeating patterns or random groupings of design and they make for speedy working in this context. When stencilling batik motifs remember the following hints. The wax should be brushed quickly over the surface of the stencil which you can then move to another position on the cloth to repeat the waxing. Speed is necessary so that the wax does not run under the edges and cause a blur on the outline of the pattern. On the other hand if you *want* a blurred, softly modulated edge

then allow the wax to flow under the tips of the stencil. This means you are using the stencil as a basis for an idea, rather than for an absolutely fixed image which cannot be changed. Stencil shapes may be used freely in this way. For instance, they can be used to make outlines leaving a central unwaxed shape clear to accept dye. Think of as many variations in the use of stencils as you can devise.

Traditionally stencils are made from pierced sheet metal but it is possible to cut them from firm cardboard. Remember that the part you cut out will be the piece that will allow wax to go onto the cloth so you must think in reverse while actually cutting the stencil itself.

A number of simple stencil shapes were cut for the wall-hanging 'Garden'. It is possible to see bands of flower clusters, each based on the use of one stencil only. Some were used on the white cloth and then were used again to protect flower shapes on each successive dye to make a variety of coloured flowers of the same strain.

The stencil shapes were also turned on themselves so that a different part of the flower was waxed at different times. This is seen clearly on the larger flowers at the bottom of the hanging. The wax was boiled off after each dyeing to facilitate this technique. Once the stencils are made this technique can go on almost indefinitely until the darkest dye is too dark to take any more. It gives multiple yet well defined shapes and colours. The stencil shapes do not have to be flower forms – they can be any shape you wish: animals, birds, fish or your own made-up abstract shapes.

Invent motifs for yourself. Do not copy these illustrations

5 Make a drawing in pastel of the first idea. This can be drawn in black on white paper.

directly. Use them as a thinking point, an incentive to experiment on your own.

To display your wall-hanging to its full advantage it should be weighted in some way so that the fabric is held taut. Turn in and sew all round the edges of the hanging and allow a turning of 2.5 cm (1 in.) top and bottom. Then simply insert a narrow dowel rod through the top and bottom hems.

Framing
Alternatively you can make your design into a wall panel by stretching the fabric across a simple frame and securing it at the back by either pinning or stapling.

ST FRANCIS
You will need:
Cotton fabric
Drawing paper
Black crayon
Tjanting
Homemade stamping blocks
Brush
Olive green, orange, pink, red and navy blue dyes

Representational work
Every branch of artistic expression divides into two broad categories: abstract and representational. If

6 Place the cloth over the black drawing so it shows through. Trace the design onto the cloth.

7 You can use a combination of methods to produce the complicated design in the background.

8 Use a tjanting to outline the finer shapes of birds and flowers and to fill in awkward areas.

you decide to attempt, say, a portrait, or to illustrate a story with figures, the way to begin is to look at the structure, shape, patterns and colour of the people around. Watch the faces of people on television, look at faces in medieval sculpture, look at newspaper photographs. Make quick sketches of ideas. Try to consider at the same time suitable backgrounds.

Work with the cloth lying on a piece of paper or on a wooden frame with the material stretched and pinned across so that wax does not drip and stick to the table surface below. The cloth should, of course, be taken off the paper, or frame, before it is dyed.

For the portrait of St Francis several batik techniques were used. The idea was drawn in black on drawing paper. It was then traced through onto the cloth. Then the waxing and dyeing process began. Careful outlining in wax was necessary to keep some of the white background sparkling through and to keep the design alive and glowing. It is generally wise to keep some white in a design as this adds a lifting quality to the pattern.

As St Francis proceeded it was decided to make the background light and the figure dark. A problem which always arises when painting or dyeing figure subjects is the colour of skin. In this case it was felt that it should not become too pink and so a mixture of very small quantities of olive green and orange was used. This combination makes a reasonable skin colour. If it is too cool for your taste, add just a touch of red.

Some of the flowers in the background were printed with the homemade blocks made for the tie section of this book. The spotty texture amongst the flowers and round the birds' wings was added

9 Dye the design flesh colour, a mixture of olive green and orange, then dry and re-wax it.

11 Change the colour of some flowers by painting on small quantities of dye with a brush.

by using the tjanting to protect small spots of colour. The nail-block was also used here.

It is possible to paint the dye onto the cloth in small areas. It must be mixed in small strong quantities with some salt and washing soda. In St Francis some of the flowers were painted in this way, their outline being protected by wax so that the painted dye did not blur at the edges. The varied colours in the background were produced by re-waxing.

When executing fine and detailed work like the St Francis hanging it is hard to prevent acci-

10 The second dye is pink. At this stage all material not covered by wax will become pink.

12 Boil off the wax in an electric washing boiler. The real quality of colour will emerge.

dental drips of wax spoiling or blurring the outline of your design. An old tin can lid or a piece of folded paper held under the tjanting as you pass it from the wax container to the design will remedy this. Or alternatively you can cut a paper surround to protect areas of the cloth.

Accidental drips can sometimes *help* the design. They can be emphasized or altered to suit your composition. If, however, they are really conspicuous, remove by first scratching off the blobs of hardened wax and then dissolving the rest with a little cleaning fluid.

Kaftan

1 Cut out template patterns from strong paper or cardboard. They can be used for repeat.

2 Place the butterfly template onto the cloth and draw around it with a soft pencil.

3 Wax the outline first and allow it to harden. This will prevent the wax spreading.

4 Allow the wax to go cold and hard then peel the cloth carefully from the backing paper.

5 Submerge the cloth immediately in the dye to get an even penetration of colour.

6 Use a lid to catch drips of wax. Wax any part of the pattern to retain the blue.

7 Submerge kaftan in yellow dye turning it constantly. Yellow on blue produces green.

8 The kaftan shows the butterflies white, part of the background blue, and the rest green.

9 Re-wax the kaftan to protect some of the green and dye for the third time in purple.

You will need:
Sufficient material to make the dress, cut out but not stitched
Strong paper or card
Pencil
Scissors
Old newspaper
Brush
Tjanting
Melted wax
Blue, yellow and purple dyes

In some crafts it is sometimes part of the design process to produce identical repeats of certain motifs. To save laborious copying it helps to make a template. This is a cut-out made from paper or cardboard which can be placed in various positions on the material and drawn round with a soft pencil. In this way the whole design can be drawn onto the cloth before waxing begins, and you can see the general shape. If alterations are necessary carry them out at the drawing stage. In this case the templates were butterflies but many other shapes can be used. They need not be natural shapes but can be triangles, hexagons or other geometric figures.

Butterfly shapes were used because they seemed to echo the general shapes of the kaftan with its large triangular shaped sleeves which suggested wings. It seemed logical that the butterflies should fly vertically in a central panel. This would make the darker ground colour on either side, and would emphasise the length of the dress rather than the width.

A kaftan was chosen because it is a simple shape to cut out and to sew and at the same time has elegance and sophistication. Cotton material was used because it is the easiest material to dye.

It is always wise to batik a garment before it is sewn together so as to allow for the shrinkage which takes place when it is boiled to remove the wax. If you decide to batik ready-made clothes, try to get a size slightly larger than you need as cotton especially is bound to shrink.

If you have enjoyed tie-dye and batik you are sure to enjoy working with wax and dyes in the exciting candlemaking projects which follow.

Introduction to Candlemaking

Making your own candles is both enjoyable and economical: anyone can learn this craft if they follow the basic rules, take a little care, and employ a little patience. It is *not* one of those crafts that demand a large initial outlay in terms of equipment: there is ample scope for the beginner in the home. The kitchen makes an ideal workroom, and glasses, mugs, yogurt jars, cans, cartons, boxes, and even paper containers can be pressed into service as moulds. All you need to buy are the basic materials – wax, wicks and dyes. One of the nicest things about candlemaking is that even if your candle is not entirely perfect, you can always melt down and re-use the materials.

Preparing the workroom
Cover the upper surface of your stove, leaving only the radiant rings or burners exposed, in a protective jacket of aluminium foil which can lift off at the end of your candlemaking session. Cover all floors and working surfaces generously with newspaper and wear old clothes and an overall. Spilled wax should be left to set and simply peeled off with the blade of a knife.

Safety
Hot wax can inflict severe burns if spilled, so make sure that the saucepan in which wax is to be melted stands firm on the burner. *Never* melt wax over a direct heat: it could over-heat and catch fire, in which case you should cover the pan with a damp cloth and switch off the heat immediately. Never pour the wax down the sink – it reacts very much like hot fat when it contacts water. Keep outside surfaces of saucepans clean and free of wax, so that there is no risk of small drips of wax catching fire and never leave melting wax unattended. Remember, too, that playing with hot wax is a dangerous activity for children.

Like any other craft, candlemaking can provide special outlets for people with individual talents such as painting, carving, appliqué work and sculpture. The beginner, however, should first master the major candlemaking techniques outlined in the projects that follow. These provide a solid basis from which to set out on your own experiments.

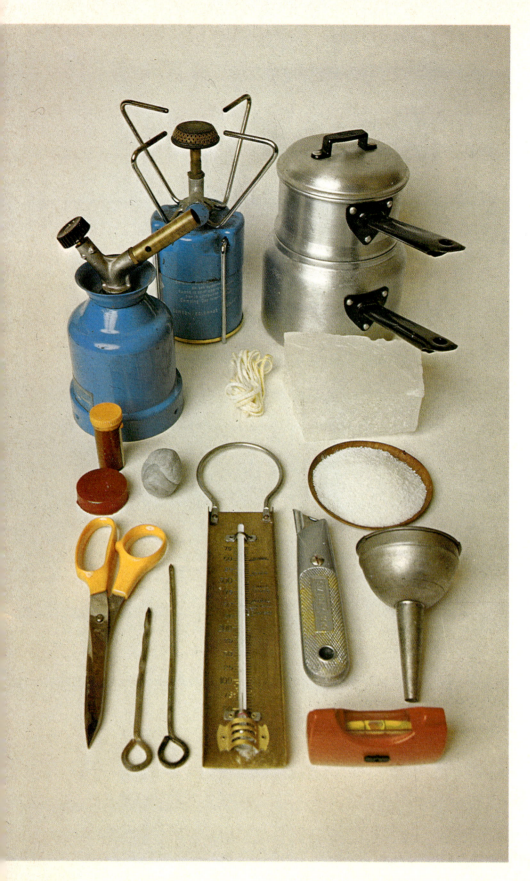

All the tools and equipment you will need to tackle the projects that follow except for the beeswax candles and sand candles. Special tools, real candlemakers' wax, dyes, wicks and moulds can be obtained from a craft store or ordered by post from major suppliers. From left to right (top row): *Camping gas stove* – useful heat source if a stove is unobtainable. *Double saucepan* – wax should always be heated over water; contact with flame can cause fire and spoil the appearance of the wax. (Second row): *Blowtorch* – any small torch will do. *Wicking* – wicks are available in various thicknesses. A candle won't burn properly unless the wick is the right size. Suppliers label wicking according to the surface diameter of the candle. Follow their recommendations carefully and keep a selection of wicks on hand. *Paraffin wax* – in block or granular form. The cheapest and most useful wax available. A small percentage of beeswax (in block form) is an excellent additive for paraffin wax. It aids even burning, gives added colour and translucence and imparts a delicious smell. (Third row): *Wax dyes* – in block or powder form. Dissolve in stearin and use sparingly. (Wax perfumes are specially formulated for adding to melted wax. Any other perfume will ruin a candle's burning quality and finish.) *Plastic clay* (or mould seal). *Stearin* (or stearic acid) – an important wax additive. It dissolves wax dyes, aids colour clarity and helps to release the candle from its mould. A good proportion of stearin to wax is 1:10. (Bottom row): *Scissors. Skewers. Sugar thermometer* – the best implement for measuring the temperature of melted wax. *Craft knife. Funnel. Spirit level* – useful for checking when making the sand candle.

Simple Moulded Candle

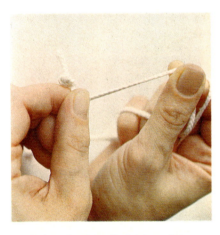

1 Take a length of wicking of the correct thickness for the mould, and knot it at one end.

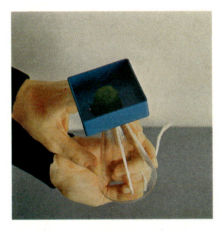

2 Thread it through the base of the mould, pull the knot taut, and seal it with plastic clay.

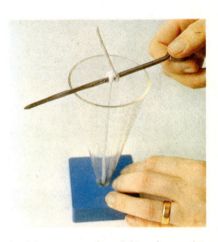

3 Now secure the wick at the top by knotting it around a skewer. It should be taut and centred.

You will need:
Paraffin wax
Stearin
Dye(s)
Wicking
Mould
2 skewers
Plastic clay, or other mould seal
Sugar thermometer
Small-lipped jug or ladle for
    pouring
Scissors or knife
Funnel for pouring (zigzag layered
    candle)

Once you have mastered the techniques illustrated over the next five pages, you are well on the way to becoming a real candle craftsman.

Moulds

Moulds need not be expensive and commercially made: it's just as good to use your own, and if it isn't possible to make a hole in the base (when, for example, you have chosen to use a cup or a glass), you can always put the wick in afterwards (see pp. 42-43).

Make sure your mould is clean and that you will be able to remove the candle from it without damaging the surface. Don't use homemade moulds which have a lip at the upper surface.

You can make your own moulds out of cardboard tubing cut to a suitable length and oiled or sprayed with a special silicone mould spray; from plastic rain-water pipe (from a building supplier), well sandpapered to remove all rough edges on the top and base edges; or from yogurt jars, waxed paper cartons, or even rolled lengths of corrugated cardboard.

Where your homemade mould has no base, improvise one out of a lid from a tin can or jar, carefully

4 Melt paraffin wax over hot water (a double boiler is ideal, but you can improvise!).

5 In another double boiler or its equivalent, melt some stearin and dissolve the chosen dye.

6 Pour in stearin and dye; at 82-93°C (180-200°F), pour into the centre of the mould.

sealed with plastic clay or commercial candlemakers' mould seal.

Wick insertion
It is sometimes helpful, if a wick is to be inserted before the wax is poured (as in these instructions) to soak the length of wicking beforehand in some white wax, and let it dry. This makes it easier for you to achieve a taut finish at the upper surface of the mould when the wick is secured. Candlemakers' suppliers sell giant 'darning needles', called wicking needles, which are also useful for threading the wick through the wick hole.

It is essential to secure the wick top and bottom absolutely firmly when preparing a mould: wicks will 'wilt' as soon as wax is poured onto them, and the greater the tension you can achieve, the better. Make sure, too, that the wick hole is properly sealed with plastic clay or mould seal to avoid molten wax dripping from the base of the mould.

Preparing wax
The wax should be heated over water. Stearin, the wax additive which encourages contraction (and therefore easy mould release) and colour brilliance, should be heated separately – again over hot water. There is no fixed formula for the addition of stearin, but less than 10% stearin in the wax will make it difficult for you to release the candle, once it has set, from its mould.

Wax dye should be added to the stearin, and the resulting mixture stirred into the melted wax. At this point, you can add a drop or two of wax perfume – but don't overdo it: they are powerful concentrates.

You will need a sugar thermometer to check the temperature of the wax/stearin/dye mixture. For a

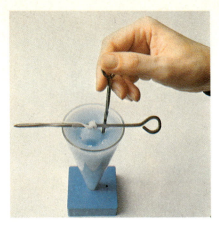

7   As the wax sets and contracts, a well forms in the centre. Pierce the surface with a skewer.

8   Reheat remaining wax to pouring temperature, and top up the candle to its original level.

9   When the candle has set, it is easy to release once the base knot has been cut.

smooth finish to the candle once it has set, it's essential to pour the wax at between 82-93° C (180-200° F). Stick to the lower temperature if your mould is glass or paper.

Try to pour the wax smoothly and evenly down the centre of the mould, as splashes down the side of the mould *could* damage the surface of the candle. When pouring is complete, tap the mould gently to release any air bubbles which may have settled in the wax.

Setting
You can set your candle in a number of ways. Perhaps the most satisfactory from the point of view of surface finish is to sink the filled mould into a bath of cold water, *to exactly the depth of the wax in the mould.* It's important to match the wax and water level, as your candle will not otherwise set and contract evenly, and you may find yourself with ugly ridges on the finished candle. With small, light candles, it isn't really feasible to use the 'water bath' method of cooling: the candle will probably float in the water unless you can weight it at the upper surface. Remember to take great care not to let any water into the candle itself: water is anathema to wax, and the finished candle probably won't burn properly.

It is nearly as good as far as smoothness of finish is concerned to simply leave the candle in a cool place, untouched, to set by itself. It takes slightly longer for a candle to set using this method, but it's certainly more convenient.

Candlemakers in a hurry can put their candles into the refrigerator to set. This really *is* a quick method, but it has its drawbacks. Firstly, the rapid temperature reduction won't allow the stearin to act as a contracting agent to the same degree as in the

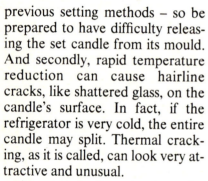

10 Prepare a mould. Melt small quantities of different coloured wax, and pour the first layer.

11 When a skin has formed, pierce holes with a skewer; pour next layer; repeat.

12 Angle the mould and alternate the angle between layers. Remove block for last layer.

previous setting methods – so be prepared to have difficulty releasing the set candle from its mould. And secondly, rapid temperature reduction can cause hairline cracks, like shattered glass, on the candle's surface. In fact, if the refrigerator is very cold, the entire candle may split. Thermal cracking, as it is called, can look very attractive and unusual.

As wax sets, it contracts, and a well forms in the centre of the candle, round the wick. You should reserve some wax in order to be able to 'top up' this well. 'Topping up', which is done again at the correct pouring temperature, is an essential procedure for a candle which will burn right to the end. Release the surface tension and anchor the new layer of wax by poking holes into the candle's surface before pouring. A perfectionist will top up more than once – and, indeed, until the surface of the candle is absolutely smooth and level.

Removing the candle
Don't be tempted to try to remove a candle from its mould until it really has had time to set. If the mould still feels very slightly warm to the touch, leave it alone.

Patience is rewarded by a smooth, shiny surface, impatience by mottles and pit marks.

Before taking the candle out of its mould, remember to remove the plastic clay or mould seal, and to cut the wick knot at the base with a knife.

Finally, gently remove the skewer, trim the wick at the base, and trim the wick at the top to a maximum of 5 mm ($\frac{1}{4}$ in.) above the candle's surface. Perfectionists conceal the wick at the base entirely, either by removing the skewer before the final topping up, or by carefully sealing it in with the judicious use of a blowtorch on the finished base surface.

Multicoloured layered candle
Accurate measurement of the *liquid* volume of a mould (do a test run with water – but dry the mould thoroughly before using it for wax) gives a solid base for an attempt at a moulded layered candle, using contrasting colours of wax. For evenly spaced layers (and providing you have a totally symmetrical mould) simply divide the total volume by the number of layers you want. Remember to melt extra wax for the top layer to allow for topping up.

Pour each layer in the normal way, at the correct temperature, and anchor each successive layer by poking holes (as for topping up) in the skinned-over previous layer with a skewer.

Use the same procedure for making zigzag layers: all you need to do apart from the above is to rest one edge of the mould base on a book or a block so that the layers set at an angle.

Lastly, if your first efforts at moulded candles are not entirely successful, don't despair: candles are amazingly economical. If you made a one-colour candle, simply melt it down, remove the wick, and store both for future use. There need be no waste at all.

If your 'failure' was a layered candle, a spatula or a flat-bladed knife may separate the layers so that you can melt these down too, and use them again. If this proves impossible, however, *don't* try to melt a multicoloured candle down *in toto:* the resulting colour will be an unappetizing muddy brown!

Whipped Wax Candle

1 Melt and dye the wax as usual, and pour it into a mixing bowl. Leave until thick skin forms.

2 Whip the wax briskly with an ordinary kitchen whisk, drawing the semi-hard wax from the sides.

3 When the wax has reached the consistency of whipped egg whites, it is ready to use.

4 Pack the mould, pressing the wax in evenly with a spatula or flat-bladed knife.

You will need:
Paraffin wax
Stearin
Dye
Wicking
Mould
Skewer
Spatula or flat-bladed knife
Egg whisk
Scissors or knife

Whipped wax makes a quick, attractive candle that needs no careful pouring. It also makes an eye-catching frosted finish for an ordinary moulded candle, and can be used to disguise the surface of moulded candle which has somehow been damaged.

The technique is very straight-forward. Simply prepare the wax/stearin/dye mixture as usual, have a mould to hand, and pour the wax into an ordinary mixing bowl. Leave it to cool until a thick skin has formed, then simply whisk it up into a light foam, rather like whipped egg whites, with a fork or whisk.

Using a spatula or a long, flat-bladed knife, pack the mould fairly speedily with the mixture, pressing it in evenly but not too firmly. Take care not to leave any holes.

5 Using a skewer, make a hole in the centre, and, again with the skewer, push a wick in.

6 Top up the candle with an extra frosting of whipped wax to seal and conceal the wick hole.

As soon as the mould is filled, pierce the centre of the candle with a skewer to form a hole for the wick, and push a wick (one that has been pre-waxed is best) into the hole. A commercial wicking needle will do the job most efficiently, but with a little care you can insert the wick through the length of the candle by simply guiding it down with the point of the skewer.

Once the wick is anchored, top up the surface of the candle with more whipped wax to seal the wick hole. Try to give the upper surface of the candle a 'frosted' finish: there's no need to have a flat, even top.

Leave the candle to set, and remove it from its mould in the normal way. The final effect will be rather like a cross-section of a cold soufflé.

If, however, the candle is not to your taste or imperfect in any way, you can disguise flaws with an extra outer frosting of whipped wax, again applied with a spatula. Remember, though, not to increase the diameter of the burning surface to the extent that the wick you have chosen is no longer suitable.

With whipped wax, you can achieve some lovely decorative effects. Using an ordinary round candle mould, cast a white candle, and don't trim the wick at the upper surface when it has been set and unmoulded. Whip some white paraffin wax and apply it with a spatula to the entire surface with the exception of the base. You'll have made a snowball candle. Trim the wick once the whipped wax has set hard. For extra effect, sprinkle glitter over soft wax.

For table centrepieces, you can anchor a group of tapers on a whipped wax base.

Carved Candle

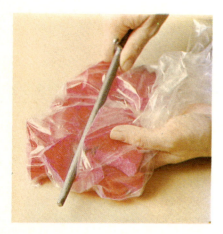

1 Take a block of pre-dyed wax and break it with a heavy instrument into small chunks.

2 Fill a prepared mould with the chunks, positioning them around the edges and in the centre.

3 Melt wax of another colour, and pour it in carefully, tapping the mould to help it flow.

4 Remove from mould when set. At this stage, it is not particularly attractive!

You will need:
Paraffin wax
Stearin
Dye
Wicking
Mould
Skewer
Sugar thermometer
Small-lipped jug for pouring
Knife
A block of pre-dyed paraffin wax
Hammer or other heavy
   instrument
Blowtorch (optional)

For all whittlers, carving wax is a very satisfying occupation. You can enhance a simple moulded candle with carvings; you can cut back the sand crust from a sand candle to show the pure wax; you can carve flowers, figures, faces, and anything at all that takes your fancy if you have the skill.

It's just a question of filling a mould with various chunks of wax, bonding them together with a contrasting coloured wax, letting the candle set, de-moulding it, and inserting a wick. When you're working with chunks, it's easier and more accurate to insert the wick after setting the candle. You can bore a central hole with a skewer (it's a slow job); or if

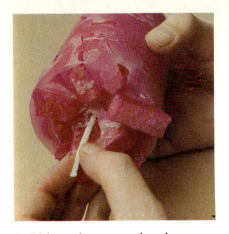

5 Using a skewer or other sharp instrument, bore a hole through the candle and insert a wick.

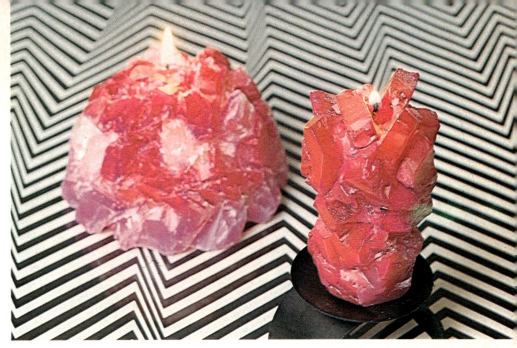

you're the owner of an electric drill, you can improvise your own extra-long drill bit out a length of thick wire (a piece cut from a wire coathanger is ideal), and this, used carefully, is a quicker method.

Simply thread the wick, pre-waxed for ease, through the hole, and seal it in at the base with your blowtorch.

No one need fear the carving process: just take a craft knife or any other sharp, short-bladed knife, and cut back the outer shell to reveal the original chunks. It's easy to do, and produces, in the end, a most attractive, rock-like finish.

If a really rough, craggy effect is what you want, there's no need at all to smooth off the edges with the blowtorch: just neaten the top surface with the blowtorch, and seal in the wick thoroughly.

Equally, if you want to achieve an even smoother effect than you can manage with the blowtorch, you can take the candle and dip it, holding the wick firmly, into a large container full of melted white paraffin wax. Hold it in the wax for a count of five, and lift it out smoothly. All angles and edges will have been softened considerably.

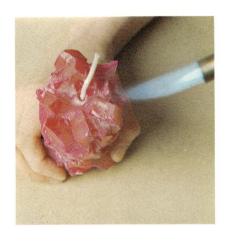

6 Seal the wick into the candle at the top with a blowtorch so that it does not show.

7 Using a craft knife, begin cutting back the wax to show the chunks.

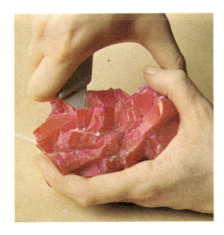

8 Continue carving until you are happy with the result. The effect should be rock-like.

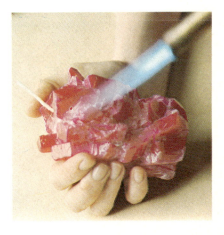

9 Soften sharp angles and knife marks gently with a blowtorch. Tidy up the top.

Sand Candles

You will need:
Paraffin wax
Stearin
Dye
Wicking
A box or bowl of sand
Small-lipped jug for pouring
Sugar thermometer
Knife
Spatula or flat-bladed knife
Blowtorch (optional)

Sand is a remarkably versatile medium for candlemaking. A homemade 'sand-pit' can be the starting point of many exciting experiments with the bonding properties of wax and sand.

Once you have mastered the technique of casting a simple shape in sand, you can embark on more ambitious projects.

The most important things to remember when working with sand are firstly to keep it damp; our childhood experiences on the beach with bucket and spade stand us in good stead: a castle made of dry sand simply collapses, but you can add all sorts of little details if you're working with wet sand. Secondly, remember that the damper the sand in your candlemaking sand-pit, the thinner the outer coating of sand on the candle will be, because the sand cools the wax quickly. Although you can overcome this to a considerable degree by pouring the wax at a high temperature (over 93° C/200° F), only practice will show you exactly how damp your sand needs to be. And thirdly, remember that any surface details in the sand mould need to be fairly bold if they are to show when the candle is unmoulded. This is not a medium for intricately detailed casting.

On the other hand, you should always sift the sand to remove any

1 Prepare a bowl of sand, dampening it so it will hold a shape pressed into it.

2 Make the surface of the sand completely flat and firm. You may like to use a spirit level.

3 Press the chosen mould shape firmly and evenly into the sand to the required depth.

lumps or stones that might spoil the finish of the candle.

If you remember these points, you will be well on the way to making some really individual and striking candles.

Variations

Once you've chosen the basic shape of a sand-moulded candle, you can alter it by creating surface bulges and indentations. Press the bowl of a spoon carefully but firmly into the sides of the sand mould to create additional surface interest, or make patterns round the upper edges by pressing a small wooden block into the sides of the mould in a repetitive pattern.

For an interesting, decorative candle, you can make legs on the outer surface of the candle by pressing lengths of dowel through the base of the mould in such a way that the candle will be able to balance on them when it is unmoulded.

You can even make two or three candles, using the same basic mould, in the sand-pit at the same time, and link them together by making a channel, like a sand castle moat, in the sand between them. Multiple-wicked candles, or joined candles like this, make stunning table decorations and give off a good light.

Of course, there's no need to leave the sand 'bowl' intact on the surface of your candle once it's unmoulded: you can cut it back to reveal the pure wax inside (it will glow rather like a pumpkin or turnip lantern as it burns): you can make patterns in the sand itself with your craft knife; or, for an extra-smooth effect, you can dip the sand casing in a bath of plain white wax.

Choosing sand

A word or two about the kind of

4 Carefully lift out the mould shape. If the impression isn't perfect, keep trying.

5 Heat the wax to a high temperature (just over 93°C/ 200°F), and pour into the mould.

6 Leave to set. Releasing the candle from its mould is just a matter of digging it out!

7 The sand crust will probably be uneven. Carve it back to a uniform thickness with a knife;

8 Bore a hole for the wick, and insert it though the centre of the candle.

9 Finally, seal in the wick at the base with a blowtorch, and neaten the upper surface too.

sand to use, and where to get it, might be helpful. The answer's easy: *any* sand will do. Sand from a beach, mixed with little fragments of shell and stone, makes lovely rough candles, but doesn't take on surface detail very easily. Your local building supplier will stock several different kinds and colours of sand – and he won't charge you much for a few small bags of it.

Finally, if you want to set aside your sand for future use once your candlemaking session is over, let it dry out thoroughly first, turning it over to let the air get right through it. Damp sand, like anything

damp, can go mouldy. Once you've dried it out, you can safely store it in airtight tins or plastic bags.

Sand moulded candle
There's a second way of using sand in candlemaking. For the less adventurous, it's easier and guarantees symmetrical results.

The basic principle of this method is to make the sand mould first in an ordinary mould – that is, to mix sand and wax together beforehand and line a mould in the same way as a cook would line a pie-dish.

It's important to work fast, as the sand/wax mixture will harden quickly. If this happens, you can soften up the mixture again by setting the bowl over hot water for a few minutes.

As in the instructions for the first method, the thickness of the sand crust is entirely up to you. This time, however, you can control it more accurately. Apply the sand/wax mixture to the base and sides of the mould, pressing it firmly and evenly against the mould wall with your fingers. It will set hard almost immediately.

You can make a hole in the

10 Prepare a mixture of sand and melted wax in a mixing bowl, stirring thoroughly to mix well.

11 Using a spatula, pack the sides of the mould; then push in the mixture.

12 Make a hole in the sand/wax base, insert and secure a wick, and fix it at the top.

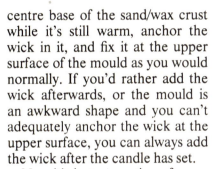

centre base of the sand/wax crust while it's still warm, anchor the wick in it, and fix it at the upper surface of the mould as you would normally. If you'd rather add the wick afterwards, or the mould is an awkward shape and you can't adequately anchor the wick at the upper surface, you can always add the wick after the candle has set.

Now it's just a question of pouring in the wax and leaving it to set as usual. You probably won't need to top up: sand and wax seem to discourage wax contraction, and you'll rarely be left with a well in the centre of the candle. Be careful not to pour the wax above the surface of the sand/wax crust, as this will spoil the outer finish; and take extra care to pour down the *centre*, as the thin sides may crumble.

Once the candle is unmoulded you need only cut back any untidy wax crust at the upper surface (and the wax in the crust as well if you want a completely smooth top), and gently soften away any knife marks with your blowtorch.

Decoration
A sand and wax mixture can also be used as surface decoration for a simple moulded candle. Apply it with a spatula, and press it on smoothly with your fingers. Untidy lines and lumps can be cut away easily afterwards when the wax has set.

Keeping clean
A word of warning about sand. . . Pockets, trouser turn-ups, handbags, and shoes, after a visit to the beach, are evidence of the incredible ability of sand to find a way into just about any container and crevice. It's no different when you're working with sand candles. You must expect a few grains of sand to loosen themselves from your mould and float in the pure wax in the centre of the candle – but you *don't* want sand in your other moulds, in nice clean wax you're using for other types of candle, or on pristine wicks. It's a good idea, therefore, to put away all your other equipment before you embark on a session of making sand candles.

13 Fill the mould with melted wax, taking extra care to pour down the centre of the mould.

14 When set, remove candle from mould, cut away excess crust, and finish with a blowtorch.

Rolled Beeswax Candle

1 Lay a suitable length of wicking along the edge of the chosen sheet of beeswax.

2 Carefully fold the edge of the beeswax sheet over the wick, securing it firmly and neatly.

3 Pressing firmly and evenly with the flat of the hands, to roll the beeswax around the wick.

You will need:
Beeswax sheeting
Wicking
Scissors or knife

Sheets of beeswax, readily available from candlemakers' suppliers, make quick, simple candles. The only trick is to keep the beeswax sheet pliable (which can be done by holding it near a heat source, or simply by holding it in a warm hand) and to roll the candle firmly and evenly.

Variations
Once you have mastered the basic technique, which is clearly shown in the step-by-step photographs, you can vary it somewhat. Use two or three sheets of wax, for example, on top of one another, and roll as before. Remember, however, to choose a thicker wick as the resulting candle will be double the thickness.

By cutting a beeswax sheet diagonally and rolling one half as usual, you can achieve a tapered effect; and a squared-up sheet rolled corner to corner will result in two tapered candles if you cut across the centre of the roll with a sharp knife.

Beeswax sheeting is so easy to work that it can be used very imaginatively for appliqué work (see page 61). The beeswax flower shown can be transformed into an attractive cake candle if at the centre of the flower you insert a tiny rolled beeswax candle.

Remnants from beeswax sheeting need not be wasted: they can be saved in tins or bags containing one colour of wax only, and used as an additive for paraffin wax.

4 Continue rolling evenly, taking care that top and base are even, until the sheet is used up.

5 Now seal the end of the sheet to the rolled candle, pressing with a finger.

6 Trim the wick, allowing about 5 mm ($\frac{1}{4}$ in.) wick to protrude; trim the base flush.

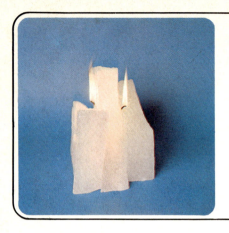

Free Form Wax Candle

You will need:
Large block of paraffin wax
Pillowcase
Hammer
Wicking
Boiling water in a bowl
Tin tray
Knife
Blowtorch

All you will need for this candle is a block of wax (cast one yourself in a roasting pan or its equivalent if you don't have one on hand), wicks, a knife, and a blowtorch.

Step-by-step, you can see that this is an easy candle to make. There are just a few points, however, worth remembering.

Firstly, unless you are working with a very thin block of wax (and this is not nearly so effective), you will need to use the thickest wicking you can find. A minimum of two wicks is necessary for the candle illustrated here, and with even four wicks the candle would burn well for a long time. For efficient burning, take a little time when the candle is finished trying to visualize just how the wicks will burn, and which surfaces they will melt first. You can sometimes im-prove the burning quality of this candle by cutting back surfaces which the flame might melt, and by carving shallow wells around the wick holes.

Secondly, try to insert the wicks as straight as possible – when you're heat-welding two blocks, this is not as easy as it sounds. If you are really having difficulty, anchor the wicks to one block first with a few dabs of glue.

It's difficult, too, to be accurate with positioning when you're heat-welding two blocks. Don't worry, though, if you've positioned the blocks inadvertently at an odd angle. The blocks are easy to pry apart with a knife – or you can simply carve away the offending wax if it's at the base and the candle won't stand level.

Once you've made the candle, you can, of course, decorate it in any way you like, although the angles and the shadows cast by the flames when the candle is burning are often sufficient decoration.

Because these candles generally don't have a completely smooth, even burning surface, they will tend to drip more than other candles. Make sure, therefore, that when you burn them you stand them on a large base.

1 Take a solid wax block – plain white paraffin wax, or coloured wax you cast yourself.

2 Put the block in an old pillowcase, and break it into chunks with a heavy hammer.

3 Take two or three of the resulting chunks, and fit them together into a shape you like.

4 Work out positions and lay the first wick along the side of a slab.

5 Melt the surface to be welded to the surface with the wick on a metal tray over hot water.

6 Quickly press down the melted surface onto the surface with the wick, and hold it down.

7 When the weld has set, seal the joins of the weld, and fill in any gaps with a blowtorch.

8 Repeat the process with the other slab, then scrape off any drip marks made by the blowtorch.

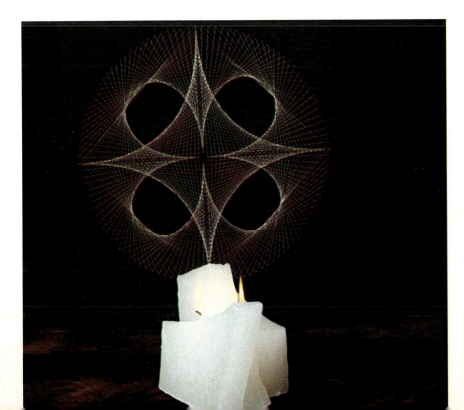

9 Trim the wicks to approximately 5 mm ($\frac{1}{4}$ in.) above the surface, and even off the base.

51

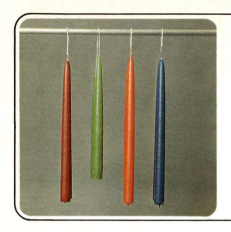

Tapers

1 Soak a suitable length of wicking in melted wax coloured to the colour of the taper.

2 Remove the wick from the melted wax, and straighten it out while it is still pliable.

3 Dip the straightened wick into a hot wax bath, very smoothly. Hold it still for five seconds.

4 Lift it out and hang it up to dry for 2 minutes. Repeat the process at regular intervals.

5 It's up to you to decide when the taper looks right. Stop dipping when you're satisfied.

6 With a sharp knife, trim off extra wax which may have gathered at the base, and trim the wick.

You will need:
Paraffin wax
Dye
Wicking
Extra-deep container for melted
   wax
Knife

The dipping technique employed in the creation of hand-made tapers is one of the oldest methods of candlemaking: tallow tapers, which have smoked and smelled away in cottages everywhere for centuries, are the forerunners of today's elegant (and much more efficient) table centrepieces.

Dipping a single taper is clearly shown in the step-by-step illustrations – but once you've tried this, you will realize why even the ancients made their tapers at least in pairs, and often in dozens.

It is a good idea to try the technique first with a single taper, though, before inventing or purchasing the equipment to manufacture in bulk.

Basically, for multiple manufacture, the number of tapers you can make at one time is determined by the depth and width of the container in which the wax is melted. A long thin container like the one pictured, is only suitable for making one taper. A deep saucepan (over a yet *larger* saucepan full of water, of course), will allow you to make two tapers at once. Tapers can be any size; long and thin or short and fat. The only limitation is the equipment you have at your disposal.

Simply knot two wicks over a length of wood, or better still a solid wooden coathanger, at a fair distance from each other. Their distance apart is determined by the diameter of the container in which the wax has been melted. If you are going to make a fat taper you will need a thicker wick than for a thin one. Proceed as for the single taper with the dip/dry process, being careful not to let them touch each other.

For multiple manufacture, a deep tin bath, or a container of some kind of sufficient depth and width is essential. Remember that your tapers can only be as long as the container is deep, and choose the vessel accordingly.

Strap, screw or nail together a lattice of wooden struts over which you can hang the individual wicks at a safe distance from each other. If possible, build a handle at a central point on this frame so that you can hold it easily. And don't forget to make provision somewhere in your workroom for the frame to hang between dippings.

Tapers need not be 'standard' in shape. Flatten them with a rolling pin shortly after a dipping when they are pliable, and twist them; plait or braid thin, soft ones together to form a taper with a triple or double wick; or make them the elaborate centrepiece of an imaginative table decoration set in a wax base (see below). You need not stand the tapers vertically as long as the base is secure so they will not fall over.

Swirled Wax Candle

You will need:
A ready-made taper
Paraffin wax
Dye
A shallow dish
Aluminium foil
A large bucket of cold water
Small-lipped jug or ladle for
    pouring

Swirled wax is a phrase that means exactly what it says: the result is an incredible array of swirls and whorls, of paper-thin fronds sweeping upwards, outwards, and around the candle.

You can swirl wax round any candle, whatever its shape or size, but as the result is delicate, a taper or a thin, simple candle is the most suitable for the purpose.

Firstly, you must set the candle in the centre of a foil-covered dish, anchoring it firmly to the centre base of the dish with a thin layer of wax. You can use wax of the same colour, or contrasting or complementary shades. Make sure the candle is absolutely vertical in the dish, or the finished article will be reminiscent of the Leaning Tower of Pisa!

Take a bucket of cold water, at least as deep as the candle itself, and put it on the floor on some

1 Cover a dish with aluminium foil. The edges of the foil should be underneath the dish.

2 Centre a candle vertically in the dish, and anchor it firmly with a layer of wax.

3 Fill up the dish with some more melted wax. Have ready a deep bucket of cold water.

4 Pick up the candle as shown and rest it gently and vertically on the surface of the water.

newspaper. Pour melted wax into the dish, up to the lip if possible, and pick up the candle (and with it, of course, the dish), holding it firmly as in the picture (see **4**). Rest the base of the dish on the surface of the water in the bucket, making sure, again, that you are keeping it absolutely vertical.

Now's the time for courage! Plunge the candle absolutely vertically into the water, twisting it around in the same movement. Hold it still for a couple of seconds, then lift it out.

The melted wax in the dish should have been forced by the movement of the water up and around the 'stem' of the candle.

It all seems fairly straightfoward as a technique . . . but there is a certain knack in plunging and twisting at the same time that you may not hit first time. It's probably better, therefore, to practise on a few old, damaged candles before attempting something really special.

To finish off a swirled wax candle, you need only peel the foil carefully from its base. You will find that, however thin the candle you have used, it will have a solid and attractive base – its own candle holder, in fact.

If you want to capitalize on the effect of 'frozen waves' which swirled wax achieves, you can decorate the base with some whipped wax, and set it with sea shells, or even simulate a 'beach' with some sand and wax built up around the base.

Swirled wax is extremely delicate, and breaks very easily. After all, it has been very finely drawn out by the force of the water. It's therefore difficult to pack and transport – and simply not suitable for sending to a cousin on the other side of the world!

5 Now plunge the candle into the water, twisting your hand (and the candle) at the same time.

6 Lift out the candle – the wax will have swirled around it. Peel off the foil.

Decorating Your Candles

There are various ways in which you can decorate a candle; but before going on to a few suggestions for simple decorative techniques, it's worthwhile saying a few general words about the principles of decorating.

It is never essential to decorate a candle. A plain candle has a beautiful simplicity of form which, coupled with clear, lovely colour and a perfect surface cannot often be bettered. You may, however, want to decorate a candle for a variety of reasons – to conceal a damaged surface, for a special occasion like a birthday, or to make a simple candle into a festive and eye-catching centre-piece for a table.

If a candle has a damaged surface (and this can happen to anyone if, for example, an insufficient quantity of stearin is used in the wax, the wax is poured at an incorrect temperature, or the mould is dirty), you can always melt it down and re-use the wax. If, however, the surface damage is not too drastic, you can save the candle by decorating it.

For festive occasions, and for gifts, the decoration can take the form of appliqués fashioned from all kinds of materials – or it may simply mean setting a simple candle in a very decorative base. There is endless scope for the imagination, but take time planning what you will do, and don't over-decorate.

Many of the decorative techniques which follow involve the use of non-wax materials. These will not melt away as the candle burns. They may also catch fire – so never decorate too close to the top of a candle and remove non-wax decorations before the candle burns down to them.

Hammering
If for any reason the surface of a candle is damaged, you can hide scratches and pit marks very easily with the hammering technique.

All you need is a suitable blunt instrument – a hammer, the handle of a spoon, or, as in the picture, a steel for sharpening knives.

Just keep hitting the surface of the candle with the chosen instrument, and try to keep the pressure at each stroke as even as possible so that a good all-over finish is achieved. Take care not to exert too much pressure or you will find that the candle itself cracks.

1 An ordinary kitchen steel for sharpening knives can be used to make attractive surface grooves.

Painting
You can paint a candle with ordinary paint (poster paint or acrylic paint), with dyed wax, or with stearin. The technique is slightly different for each of these media.

Paint
It's easiest of all to use ordinary paint and a brush on a candle's surface. Just paint on your chosen design, and leave it to dry. Paint is the ideal medium for intricate designs, too, and if you're good with a brush you can achieve little works of art.

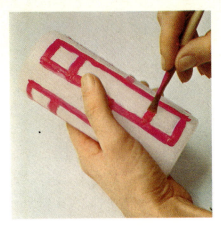

2 Acrylic paint can be used straight from the tube but moistened slightly with water.

3 Using a paintbrush and some warm paraffin wax, work quickly to achieve a painted effect.

4 Take a teaspoon and some warmed stearin and dye mixture, and trickle it onto the candle.

Paraffin wax

Paraffin wax is also applied with a paintbrush, but the problem with painting with wax is that it dries almost the instant that the brush touches the candle – so you have to work fast!

Keep the wax you are using for painting warm over hot water; and to help to paint the pattern quickly but accurately, lightly draw in the design on the candle's surface with a soft pencil or a crayon before beginning work with the melted wax.

Of course, stearin and dye may simply be melted together and applied with a paintbrush too. But because the colour of a pure stearin/dye mixture is so brilliant, you can also drip it onto the candle's surface.

Transfers

The advent of rub-down lettering has opened up a great new vista of beautifully printed, brightly coloured pictorial transfers which can be applied, in the same way as instant lettering, to just about any surface – including candles.

It's quick, clean, and easy to apply these transfers. Try to use a flat-edged spatula (obtainable from art suppliers) to do the rubbing-on. Don't press harder than is absolutely necessary, as your rubbing marks may show on the surface of the candle. You can dip the candle into wax to seal the transfer but it's not essential, and you'll dull those brilliant colours.

Don't try to use the old-fashioned kind of transfer or decal that has to be dampened with water. Even if it *will* stick to the surface, it's a bad idea in case any water gets trapped against the candle's surface. Water in the wax is the fastest possible way to make a candle splutter and go out.

5 That eternally-popular Walt Disney character Donald Duck has been transferred to this candle.

Appliqué

One of the most fruitful and interesting ways of decorating a candle is to use appliqués of one kind or another. The range is tremendous, and the photographs here illustrate only a few possibilities.

Try your hand first at the simplest techniques before attempting more complicated methods.

Paper appliqué

Illustrated here is the simplest of all forms of appliqué: sticking on those round adhesive paper price tags to represent the spots on a dice. Using these same adhesive price tags, you can build up multicoloured patterns on the candle's surface.

Cut-outs

You can cut out suitable pictures for decorating a candle from old Christmas and birthday cards, magazines, posters, and books – a picture of Santa Claus for a Christmas candle, for example, or a pretty bunch of flowers – and glue them carefully to the candle. One quick dip in melted white paraffin wax will make the candle look more professional.

You can cut your own shapes and patterns out of paper, and glue and dip them in the same way.

Glueing motifs to the candle's surface is easy to do, and offers many possibilities.

Christmas decorations

Save small seasonal decorations to give you instant seasonal candles next year.

Simply choose a decoration whose colours complement that of the candle, and glue it on.

Commercial decorations, such as holly and flower sprigs, are available all year round from shops which sell cake decorating equipment.

Glitter

You can buy little tubes of commercial glitter very easily, especially at Christmas time. Use it to give life to an otherwise dull candle – simply glue it onto the surface – or combine it with other effects, like whipped wax, to give an extra sparkle to the finished decoration.

Sequins

Sequins are another way of bringing a little sparkle into your

1 Stick little adhesive labels on the surface of a square candle to simulate the spots on a dice.

2 Glue the back of the Christmas decoration firmly to the surface of the candle.

3 Stroke a thin, even layer of glue over the surface of the candle to be decorated.

4 Sprinkle the glitter onto the glue-covered surface while the glue is still tacky.

5 Shake off the excess gently. Some glitter will remain on the surface in the pattern you drew.

6 Press sequins gently but firmly against the surface of this diagonally-rolled beeswax taper.

candles. The method illustrated is only one way in which they can be used. You can also glue sequins in patterns directly onto the candle's surface or use them with glitter to achieve a really sumptuous, sparkling effect.

With beeswax, as illustrated, it isn't so easy to glue appliqués to the honeycomb surface. With light, sharp-edged objects such as sequins, it's often enough just to press them into the surface firmly but carefully, and they will adhere. They are simple to remove, too, when the candle burns down. For more detailed appliqué work on

beeswax, it's easiest to pin your decoration into the candle with tiny pins.

Sea shells

Sea shells are lovely in candle light and make a delightful addition to a plain candle base.

A large, flat piece of mother of pearl, set upright in a base behind a candle, will look absolutely stunning.

Sea shells glued in patterns to the surface of the candle can be just as attractive; and the idea illustrated shows how a simple taper, some white whipped wax, and shells can be combined to form a beautiful table centrepiece.

Leaves and everlasting flowers

Small, flat leaves from plants, fern fronds, petals and flat-dried flowers all make excellent appliqués. Glue them lightly in position on the candle's surface and give the candle a final dip in white paraffin wax. This seals in the appliqués, helps retain their colour and stops the edges curling.

Everlasting flowers can be bought singly, by the head, from your florist and make useful and attractive candle decorations. Dipping each head once in

7 Build up a base of whipped wax with a spatula around an ordinary taper.

8 While the whipped wax is still soft, press in shells as decoration and to steady the base.

9 Glue the leaf all over one side, and fix it firmly to the surface of the candle.

10 Dip the candle in white paraffin wax to seal the leaf so its edges won't curl.

11 Pass a pin through the centre of a dried flower-head, and push the pin into the candle.

12 Carefully glue tiny wax chunks in a pattern to the surface of your chosen candle.

13 When the glue has dried, dip the candle smoothly, once, into melted wax to soften the edges.

paraffin wax before fixing them to the candle gives a waxy sheen.

Although it is easy to glue everlasting flowers to the surface of a paraffin wax candle they can be hard to remove as the candle burns. An equally attractive and safer method of application is to simply pin the flower to the softer surface of a beeswax candle.

Wax chunks

The small chunks of wax left over from making a carved candle can be kept and re-used as appliqués. Simply glue really small chunks in a pattern of your choosing to the surface of the candle.

If you like, you can soften off the edges with a blowtorch (being careful not to let the chunks drip), or dip the whole candle just once into melted wax, white or coloured, to make the chunks look an integral part of the candle.

Beeswax sheets

Beeswax sheets are easy to use for making actual candles – and nearly as easy and quick to use in candle appliqué work.

As it is so soft and pliable, it can be plaited, cut, rolled, and sculpted in whatever shape takes your fancy.

When gluing a beeswax appliqué, unless the honeycomb effect has been ironed out, it is important to make sure every little cavity in the honeycomb is well-glued so the appliqué will stick.

Paraffin wax

Paraffin wax lacks the pliability of beeswax, and therefore has to be kept soft over (or even in) hot water before use as appliqué.

The technique illustrated for beeswax appliqué also applies to paraffin wax, although you will have to pour and set your own thin sheet of wax to begin with. If the resulting sheet is kept warm,

14 Using a flat-based tin or plate, pour a thin layer of paraffin wax to form a sheet.

15 Place the tin over a bowl of hot water to keep the wax pliable. Cut strips from the sheet.

16 Place the strips in a bowl of warm water so they will keep soft till you need them.

17 Pre-glue the candle; at the moment of fixing, twist the strips and press them on.

18 Cut out shapes from a sheet of beeswax with confectioners' candy cutters.

19 Glue the shapes carefully to the candle, making certain that they are covered with glue.

20 Cut petal shapes, of varying sizes, from a sheet of modelling wax. They need not be accurate.

21 Work a small petal shape into something nearer to nature, and build up the flower shape.

22 Add a tiny 'pistil' to the flower with a ball of contrasting modelling wax, using a needle.

23 Press leaves firmly to flower base. Work wax at flower base to fix to the candle.

you can cut shapes either with confectioners' cutters or freehand just as easily, and they can be kept pliable if they are floated on the surface of a bowl of warm water until you are ready to use them. Remember to dry them off on a little absorbent paper before applying them.

Modelling wax

As its name implies, modelling wax is a special formulation of waxes, bought in thin sheets, which can be bent, cut, moulded, and sculpted in any way.

Kept away from direct heat, it remains hard; but as soon as your hand warms it, it becomes as pliable as plastic clay (and much less sticky to work with).

A little imagination, and some patient working with the fingers, will give you the effect illustrated.

Modelling wax (and indeed beeswax, which can be worked in the same way – although not so easily) can be made into flower shapes, into tiny houses, into snowmen, into animal shapes and can persuade you that you'll never waste money buying commercial cake candles again. With a little ingenuity, you can work a wick into the chosen shape and with modelling wax there's no difficulty at all in achieving detail.

For an original gift, you can work a candle in the shape of a red rose: roll a tiny candle for the centre of a rose (remember to use an equally tiny wick), and build up the petals around it. Fix the flower base into tiny green leaves (it's best to have a picture of a rose in front of you for this), and push the flower into a length of strong wire (again, wire coat-hangers are very useful).

Build up the flower stem with brown modelling wax, working up thorns with your fingers, and adding little leaf buds.

LIST OF SUPPLIERS

Great Britain

Dyes

Dylon International Ltd
Oxford Works
Worsley Bridge Road
London SE 26

Golden Tortoise
11a Westgate
Ripon
Yorkshire

Reeves and Co.
Enfield
Middlesex

Candle Makers' Supplies
4 Beaconsfield Terrace Road
London W14

Ciba Geigy (UK) Ltd (suede dyes)
Ullswater Crescent
Coulsdon
Surrey
and
Clayton
Manchester

Wax

Candle Makers' Supplied
4 Beaconsfield Terrace Road
London W14

The Candles Shop
89 Parkway,
London NW1

Tjantings and brushes

Dryads Handicrafts Ltd
Northgates
Leicester

U.S.A.

Aljo Manufacturing Co. Inc.
116 Prince Street
New York, New York 10012

Keystone-Ingham Co.
13844 Struikman Road
Cerritos, California 90701

Screen Process Supplies
1199 East 12th Street
Oakland, California 94606

Stephen Blumrich
Ronte 1, Box 25a
Halsey, Oregon

Dick Blick Art Materials
P.O. Box 1267
Galesburg, Illinois 61401

Dadant and Sons, Inc.
Hamilton, Illinois 62341

Mobile Oil Company
612 S. Flower
Los Angeles, California 90065

Sax Art & Crafts
207 N. Milwaukee St.
Milwaukee, Wisconsin 53202

Art Brown & Bros. Inc.
2 West 46th Street
New York, New York 10036

J. C. Larson Co., Inc.
7330 N. Clark Street
Chicago, Illinois 60626

Pourette Mfg. Co.
6818 Roosevelt Way N.E.
Seattle, Washington 98115

Celebration Candle Supplies
P.O. Box 28
Pentwater, Michigan 49448

Earth Guild/Grateful Union
149 Putnam Avenue
Cambridge, Massachussetts 02139

Craftool Co. Inc.
1421 West 240th Street
Harbor City, California 90710

SOME FURTHER READING

Batik: Art and Craft, Nit
Krevitsky, Studio Vista, London,
1968; Van Nostrand Reinhold,
New York, 1968

*Batik: Materials, Technique,
Design,* Sara Nea, Van Nostrand
Reinhold, New York, 1971

Batik: The Art and Craft, Keller,
Prentice Hall, London; Tuttle,
Tokyo

Batik for Beginners, Norma
Jameson, Studio Vista, London,
1970; Watson-Guptill, New York

*Batik, Tie Dyeing and Fabric
Printing,* French and Schrapel,
Hale, London

Batiks, John Irwin and Veronica
Murphy, Victoria and Albert
Museum, London, 1969

The Book of Batik, Muehling,
Mills and Boon, London;
Taplinger, New York

Contemporary Batik and Tie-Dye,
Dona Z. Meilach, Allen and
Unwin, London

Introducing Batik, Evelyn Samuel,
Batsford, London, 1969;
Watson-Guptill, New York

Tie Dye, Sara Nea, Van Nostrand
Reinhold, New York, 1971

*Tie and Dye as a Present Day
Craft,* Anne Maile, Mills and
Boon, London, 1963

Tie Dye Made Easy, Anne Maile,
Mills and Boon, London;
Taplinger, New York

The Complete Candlemaker, Ann
Hirst-Smith, Studio Vista 1974;
Watson Gupthill, New York.

Getting Started in Candlemaking,
Walter Schutz, Bruce Publishing
Co., London 1972; Collier Books,
New York.

Creative Candlecraft, Joan Ann
Unger, Grosset and Dunlap, New
York 1972.

64